ALICE IN WONDERLAND

In a new version by
Jack Bradfield and Poltergeist

Lyrics by Gerel Falconer

Copyright © 2022 by Poltergeist and Jack Bradfield, Gerel Falconer
Illustration by Israel Kujore, Graphic Design by Guy J Sanders
All Rights Reserved

ALICE IN WONDERLAND is fully protected under the copyright laws of the British Commonwealth, including Canada, the United States of America, and all other countries of the Copyright Union. All rights, including professional and amateur stage productions, recitation, lecturing, public reading, motion picture, radio broadcasting, television, online/digital production, and the rights of translation into foreign languages are strictly reserved.

ISBN 978-0-573-13375-6
concordtheatricals.co.uk
concordtheatricals.com

FOR AMATEUR PRODUCTION ENQUIRIES

UNITED KINGDOM AND WORLD
EXCLUDING NORTH AMERICA
licensing@concordtheatricals.co.uk
020-7054-7298

Each title is subject to availability from Concord Theatricals, depending upon country of performance.

CAUTION: Professional and amateur producers are hereby warned that *ALICE IN WONDERLAND* is subject to a licensing fee. The purchase, renting, lending or use of this book does not constitute a licence to perform this title(s), which licence must be obtained from the appropriate agent prior to any performance. Performance of this title(s) without a licence is a violation of copyright law and may subject the producer and/or presenter of such performances to penalties. Both amateurs and professionals considering a production are strongly advised to apply to the appropriate agent before starting rehearsals, advertising, or booking a theatre. A licensing fee must be paid whether the title is presented for charity or gain and whether or not admission is charged.

This work is published by Samuel French, an imprint of Concord Theatricals Ltd.

The Professional Rights in this play are controlled by Independent Talent, 40 Whitfield St, London W1T 2RH.

No one shall make any changes in this title for the purpose of production. No part of this book may be reproduced, stored in a retrieval system, scanned, uploaded, or transmitted in any form, by any means, now known or yet to be invented, including mechanical, electronic, digital, photocopying, recording, videotaping, or otherwise, without the prior written permission of the publisher. No one shall share this title, or part of this title, to any social media or file hosting websites.

The moral right of Jack Bradfield, Poltergeist and Gerel Falconer to be identified as author(s) of this work has been asserted in accordance with Section 77 of the Copyright, Designs and Patents Act 1988.

USE OF COPYRIGHTED MUSIC

A licence issued by Concord Theatricals to perform this play does not include permission to use the incidental music specified in this publication. In the United Kingdom: Where the place of performance is already licensed by the PERFORMING RIGHT SOCIETY (PRS) a return of the music used must be made to them. If the place of performance is not so licensed then application should be made to PRS for Music (www.prsformusic.com). A separate and additional licence from PHONOGRAPHIC PERFORMANCE LTD (www.ppluk.com) may be needed whenever commercial recordings are used. Outside the United Kingdom: Please contact the appropriate music licensing authority in your territory for the rights to any incidental music.

USE OF COPYRIGHTED THIRD-PARTY MATERIALS

Licensees are solely responsible for obtaining formal written permission from copyright owners to use copyrighted third-party materials (e.g., artworks, logos) in the performance of this play and are strongly cautioned to do so. If no such permission is obtained by the licensee, then the licensee must use only original materials that the licensee owns and controls. Licensees are solely responsible and liable for clearances of all third-party copyrighted materials, and shall indemnify the copyright owners of the play(s) and their licensing agent, Concord Theatricals Ltd., against any costs, expenses, losses and liabilities arising from the use of such copyrighted third-party materials by licensees.

IMPORTANT BILLING AND CREDIT REQUIREMENTS

If you have obtained performance rights to this title, please refer to your licensing agreement for important billing and credit requirements.

The script was correct at the time of printing, but may differ to what is presented on stage.

ALICE IN WONDERLAND was first produced by Brixton House and Poltergeist Theatre, on 1st December 2022 at Brixton House. The cast was as follows:

ALICE	Nkhanise Phiri
QUEEN OF THE LINE / CHATTER / MUM	Toyin Ayedun-Alase
RABBIT / PIGEON / HAMMERSMITH	Khai Shaw
TORTOISE / DUM / RAT / DISTRICT	Rosa Garland
CAT / DEE / NOSE / CIRCLE	Will Spence

CREATIVE TEAM

Director and Lead Writer	Jack Bradfield
Composer and Sound Designer	Alice Boyd
Set Designer and Co-Graphic Designer	Shankho Chaudhuri
Costume Designer	Debbie Duru
Producer for Poltergeist	Emily Davis
Lyricist and Rapperturg	Gerel Falconer
Production Manager	Ethan Hudson
Illustrator and Co-Graphic Designer	Israel Kujore
Lighting Designer	Rajiv Pattani
Costume Supervisor	Isobel Pellow
Dance Captain	Khai Shaw
Fight Director	Rebecca Wilson
Fight Director	Lucy Wordsworth
Company Stage Manager	Chloe Ashley
Deputy Stage Manager	Chloe Astleford
Assistant Stage Manager	Gracie Adlington
LX Programmer	Gareth Weaver
Scenic Painters	Jakub Kury
	Ilaria Ciardelli
	Jessica Perkins

CHARACTERS

ALICE
QUEEN OF THE LINE, CHATTER, MUM
RABBIT, PIGEON, HAMMERSMITH
TORTOISE, DUM, RAT, DISTRICT
CAT, DEE, NOSE, CIRCLE

AUTHOR'S NOTES

Welcome to Wonderland

We wanted Wonderland to be a living breathing world. We wanted audiences to feel like for every scene happening on stage, there were three others happening somewhere just out of sight. We wanted to take Carroll's Alice stories and remix them for right here and right now.

So, meet Alice. She's an eleven-year-old girl from Brixton. She writes lyrics, she's starting a new school, and she absolutely does not get on with her Mum. Brixton Underground Station is our Rabbit Hole, a Victoria Line tube train is our Wonderland.

Our *Alice in Wonderland* is the result of two years of workshops with a fantastic creative team of illustrators, lyricists, designers, and composers. Making work this way was a bold step for us, and one I'm proud we took.

This show has been all about the collaboration. I remember Israel our Illustrator sketching a version of the Cheshire Cat – a lonely hacker in a hoodie – that felt so spot on he had to go right in the show. I remember seeing Gerel our lyricist and Alice our composer disappear in a musical fever and return thirty minutes later with the central song of the play, Alice-tocracy. I remember sitting down with Debbie our costume designer and discussing how interesting it might be if the Hatter and the Queen were played by the same actor. Every decision we make in rehearsal is built on a deep foundation of collaborative creative thought.

We're drawing from so much that excites us as a company. We're inspired by Brixton, of course, making a show specifically for the House this Christmas. We're inspired by anime and comic-books, our way of bringing Alice's visual world right into the present day. We're inspired by the London Underground, a strange in-between space, full of particular personalities; a portal that takes us across the city. And then we're taking our lead from the spirit of the book itself – this show is packed with easter-eggs from the original story, so keep your eyes peeled.

Alice in Wonderland has been a joy to make. We've had the most fantastic cast, all brimming with ideas, all precise, funny, and serious about making this show the best it can be. Every day there's a new rabbit hole to fall down, a new discovery to be made.

Alice steps on a train headed to Wonderland. It's a change to the schedule – a disruption – but you know what? I'd say after the past few years, young people are well prepared to handle a bit of nonsense.

A note on the text:
This text has been created from a series of workshops with actors and creatives, including: Toyin Ayedun-Alase, Alice Boyd, Shankho Chaudhuri, Angelina Chudi, Debbie Duru, Emily Davis, Doxah Dzidzor, Janet Etuk, Gerel Falconer, Rosa Garland, Anne Odeke, Kwami Odoom, Israel Kujore, Rajiv Pattani, Nkhanise Phiri, Khai Shaw, and Will Spence.

A forward slash (/) marks the point of interruption of overlapping dialogue.

Text in square brackets like [this] indicates a word a character is intending to say, but does not.

ACT ONE

One

(Brixton Underground Station. **MUM** *is carrying a box of Christmas things – tinsel, stars, a few presents.* **ALICE** *holds a paper tube map, and works out some lyrics.)*

ALICE.
EVERYONE LISTEN UP GATHER ROUND
I AM THE BRAND NEW... ACTON TOWN
SOON I'LL BE BIGGER THAN... MANOR HOUSE
I'VE GOT MORE LINES THAN THE UNDERGROUND

Have you got a rhyme for *Underground*?

MUM. Can we do this later Alice –

ALICE. I don't want to go.

MUM. Well you have to go.

ALICE. Do you know how much a tube fare is now.

MUM. *It's free.*

ALICE. No it's not, / I'm eleven I have a *Zip card*.

MUM. Well how much is it?

ALICE. 85p.

MUM. 85p, I am *okay with 85p for you to see your /grandmother.*

ALICE. And I've got *homework*.

*(**MUM** snorts.)*

What? Why are you laughing.

MUM. I'm not laughing.

ALICE. You are, you did a – a – *(**ALICE** snorts.)*

MUM. Well you won't be doing it you'll be lying on your bed on your phone, / writing bars –

ALICE. *Why are you spying on me?*

MUM. I'm not spying on you. What is it then?

ALICE. English.

MUM. The whole language?

*(We hear the loud screech of a tube train on the other platform. **ALICE** jumps.)*

ANNOUNCER. Apologies Ladies and Gentlemen there are signal failures this / evening further up the line. Please bear with us.

MUM. What are you doing for *English*?

*(**ALICE** pulls out the book.)*

ALICE. *Alice in Wonderland.*

MUM. You're named after her, you know.

ALICE. Really?

MUM. Ha. *No.* You're named after Alice Cooper.

ALICE. Who's that?

MUM. *Schools Out For Summer!*

ALICE. *Shush.*

MUM. Tell me what you think then.

ALICE. I think you're the worst singer I've ever heard.

MUM. Of *Alice in Wonderland* –

ALICE. Oh. It's terrible.

MUM. *Why?*

ALICE. Because it is.

MUM. *Use your English.*

ALICE. Because it's this girl who thinks she's perfect, and goes around telling everyone else what to do. And that's it, that's literally the whole thing.

MUM. Sounds familiar.

ALICE. And it has a rubbish ending. Because it's all a dream. Which is the worst ending ever. *Oh no I've written a whole thing that makes no sense so I guess it's a dream then –*

(**MUM***'s scrolling on her phone.*)

And you're not even listening to me.

MUM. Sorry – work –

ALICE. I thought I was at Dad's tonight anyway –

MUM. Well your Dad and I were talking and we both thought it might be nice for you to see Nani, to *connect*. So that's what we're doing. And we're not arguing.

ANNOUNCER. The next Victoria Line service to Walthamstow Central / will arrive in one minute. One minute. Thank you.

MUM. Hold my hand.

ALICE. No.

MUM. We hold hands on the tube.

(*She reaches again.* **ALICE** *moves her hand.*)

Alice don't be silly.

(*Beat. She reaches again.*)

ALICE. *STOP*. You don't need to [hold my hand] –

MUM. Alice. We hold hands. It matters.

ALICE. Why does it matter?

MUM. Because I'm your Mum, Alice, god I don't know! Why are you being like this? You've been in a bad mood all day –

ALICE. So have you – you have been so mean all week.

MUM. I haven't.

ALICE. YOU HAVE!

MUM. Honestly, I'm this close to walking away and getting the train in the other direction.

ALICE. You can't do that.

MUM. And why can't I?

ALICE. Brixton is the end of the line, *there's NOTHING IN THE OTHER DIRECTION*.

MUM. How mature… I expect more from someone in secondary school – you're locking yourself in your room, / and actually I understand why you're not having any friends over if you're acting like this – I feel like we're trapped in a – in a – / loop –

ALICE. I'm not! That's only because you – you –

STOP!

MUM. Alice there are people around –

> *(The **TRAIN** pulls up. The doors open. **MUM** reaches for **ALICE**'s hand.)*

ALICE. Leave. Me. ALONE.

> *(**ALICE** slaps it away.)*

MUM. Right you are in big trouble.

(**ALICE** *makes to get on the train.* **MUM** *grabs her arm.*)

No. You're not getting on that train. We are going to have a talk right here, right now.

(**ALICE**, *tears in her eyes. Steps backwards, onto the tube, just as the doors shut.*)

MUM. Get off at the next station. Meet me at the next station. Alice. ALICE!

(The train pulls away.)

Two

> (**ALICE** is on the tube. Near her sits a **BUSINESSMAN**, face hidden behind a newspaper.)
>
> (**ALICE** is fuming. She turns up her headphones. Music blares in her ears.)
>
> (Text on the LED Screen: 'Next stop: STOCKWELL'.)
>
> (She takes out her phone, and starts muttering lyrics to herself.)

ALICE.
ALICE-TOCRACY, ALICE-STOCRACY,
I'M THE QUEEN OF THE SOUND NOTHIN'S STOPPIN' ME.
ALICE-TOCRACY, ALICE-STOCRACY,
I'M THE BEST AND THERE'S NO MEDIOCRITY.

> (The tube jolts. Stops. Then suddenly begins to speed up. Faster and faster. Sparks fly. **ALICE** holds on tight.)
>
> (Then suddenly, the lights cut out.)
>
> (The lights flicker back on.)

(To the **BUSINESSMAN**.) Er. Excuse me.

Excuse me?

I was just wondering when we're getting to the next –

MAN. *Shh.*

> (Beat.)

ALICE. I'd just like to know when's the next stop.

MAN. Shh.

ALICE. I'm –

MAN. Shhhh.

ALICE. Alright, suit yourself.

>   *(Long pause.)*

>   *All I'm asking is –*

MAN. You can't ask me anything.

ALICE. *Why not!*

>   *(The newspaper whips down. This is no man. This is a **RABBIT**. Long white ears, business attire, bright white sneakers.)*

RABBIT. *BECAUSE YOU'RE NOT MEANT TO BE HERE.*

Besides, I'm late. Time is *precious* and you're draining it out of me like a leaky *Waterloo*.

ALICE. You're a! YOU'RE A –

RABBIT. Fine, shout if you want. Not my fault if you get *eaten*.

ALICE. *(Going through rhymes to calm herself down.)* Rabbit – habit – grab it – err – tablet –

RABBIT. No rhymes on the line!

>   *(**ALICE** starts clapping in front of her face.)*

And what's *this?!*

ALICE. TRYING TO WAKE UP.

RABBIT. This isn't a dream. And I'll tell you whyfor!

>   *(The **RABBIT** shows **ALICE** his newspaper.)*

Look how far the Stockwell market's crashed this morning. If anything, it's a nightmare!

>   *(The tube tannoy screeches:)*

QUEEN. Good evening one and all! And what an evening it is, still on the train, still heading exactly where we need to go. I would like to remind everyone, as I do every evening, to please remain in your carriages. Anyone breaking the rules will have to answer to my *Jabberwocky*, who will of course see it, *slay it*, sort it.

Have a lovely night, and remember, we're *right on track*.

> (**RABBIT** *joins in on 'right on track'. The tannoy cuts out.*)

RABBIT. There, you see. If *The Queen of the Line* finds I've got a *Walthamstowaway* I'm in big trouble. Go back to your own carriage.

ALICE. My own carriage?

RABBIT. Yes. We stick to our own carriage. That's the rules.

ALICE. I don't have *a carriage*.

RABBIT. You're pulling my foot.

ALICE. I just got on.

RABBIT. You're an... oh *no*... you're an *OVER-GROUNDER*?

ALICE. I'm from Brixton.

RABBIT. *BRIXTON*. This is worse than I thought!

ALICE. I just want to know *when's the next stop*.

RABBIT. Stop? We don't stop. That's why I'm in such a rush.

> (*A zip of orange energy leaps around the carriage. It jumps into* **RABBIT**'s *phone, which buzzes.*)

PHONE. Meow.

RABBIT. No no no. Get out. Get out. GET OUT.

(He hits the phone hard enough to send the light bouncing out of the phone, and away toward another carriage.)

ALICE. ...what was that?

RABBIT. It was the *Cat*.

ALICE. In your phone?

*(**ALICE** rushes over to a shape on the other side of the carriage. This is a Commuter – a shadow of a person, sucked of life and curiosity.)*

Excuse me. This rabbit is chatting rubbish and I need to get off. Hello?

*(The Commuter turns to **ALICE**, a blank, hollow look.)*

RABBIT. I wouldn't waste a second with that one. It won't talk to you.

ALICE. *(Trying again.)* HELLO. Please?

RABBIT. That's a *Commuter*.

ALICE. A Commuter?

RABBIT. A Commuter. If you spend too long on a train, you become one. You lose all hope. Luckily that will never happen to me, because I'm going the Queensway! She's taking us exactly where we need to go. I think we're going to *an office. I know. Exciting!*

*(**ALICE** looks about anxiously.)*

Look, there might be some others on the train that can help you. Maybe try another carriage.

*(**ALICE** makes to go.)*

Not that way, it's haunted.

ALICE. *Haunted?!*

RABBIT. Yes, on a dark Knightsbridge ghosts escaped from Mansion House. *That way to the front.*

> (**ALICE** *puts her hand on the door, but backs off.*)

You could wait here until the Queen finds you – but be warned – girls caught fare far worse than Earls Court.

> (**ALICE** *steps forward, the distance between this carriage and the next stretches out in front of her. Wind blowing her hair, the door glowing on the other side. Between her and the next carriage is a strange, mysterious portal. His voice echoes across the darkness:*)

Oh, and…

Mind The Gap!

> (**ALICE** *stands on the threshold.*)

ALICE. Are you sure this is… the only way?

RABBIT. *(Calling, offstage.)* QUITE SURE.

ALICE. Alright… deep breath.

> (**ALICE** *breathes in, steps back, and leaps.*)

Three

*(A carriage with a **HOLIDAYMAKER**, a bucket hat and suitcases.)*

ALICE. Oh, hi! Hello! I'm wondering when the next stop is.

(One of the suitcases starts barking at her.)

AAAAA!

(Then another, then another!)

HOLIDAYMAKER. *(Over the noise.)* SORRY, I GOT ON AT BARKING.

(She's out the door.)

***

*(A **WOMAN** cradles a mobile phone like a baby.)*

ALICE. Hi, excuse me miss –

WOMAN. Ssssshhhh, I just got her to sleep.

ALICE. Got who to sleep?

WOMAN. The Baby!

ALICE. What Baby?

(The phone starts crying loudly –)

WOMAN. Look what you did.

*(**ALICE** screams and runs on.)*

***

(A carriage full of **CONCERT GOERS**, *singing along, waving glow sticks.)*

ALL.
VICTORIA LINE, IT'S THE BEST LINE IN THE WORLD
SO GOOD, SO GOOD, SO GOOD

*(**ALICE** pushes through to the next carriage.)*

***

*(A Commuter sits there... and stares at **ALICE** as she passes.)*

***

*(A **GIANT** stomps through the carriage.)*

GIANT. Excuse me please.

*(**ALICE** lets the **GIANT** pass, and moves on.)*

***

*(**ALICE** lands in a tiny carriage, too small for her.)*

(She begins to make her way through the carriage.)

(We hear the screaming of tiny people.)

ALICE. Excuse me. Sorry. Excuse me. Coming though. Coming through!

(She accidentally steps on something. The crowd go silent.)

Are you... okay?

LITTLE VOICE. I'm okay! Just don't do it again!

(She struggles forward again.)

ALICE. I'm stuck. I can't move –

>*(Chatter.)*

What did you say? Oi. *Don't be rude*. Wait, what are you doing? Wait. WAIT!

>*(A rally cry! Three! Two! One!)*

Woaaaaaah!

>*(**ALICE** is thrown forward into.)*

>*****

>*(A **POSH COUPLE** clutching* Alice in Wonderland *programmes.)*

POSH WOMAN. Dear, do you know how to get to *Brixton House*?

POSH MAN. *There's a play on there.* Apparently it's for *(Disgusted.) young people.*

POSH WOMAN. But you've got to get your culture, *(Rabid.)* you've *got to get your culture!*

POSH MAN. You do you've GOT TO GET YOUR CULTURE –

ALICE. What are you guys?

BOTH. We're Culture Vultures… squawk!

ALICE. I think I saw some culture that way!

>*(They look away, while **ALICE** legs it out of there.)*

***

(And into a carriage full of protesters. All holding placards.)

PROTESTOR. Just stop!

ALICE. What?

PROTESTOR. Down with the thing.

ALICE. Oh.

PROTESTOR. What do we want? Break the loop…

ALICE. What loop?

PROTESTOR. Just stop.

Down with the thing.

*(The **PROTESTER** repeats and repeats the slogans.)*

Four

(A carriage made up a like a football pitch.)

*(**DUM** and **DEE** stand at either end of the carriage, 'in goal'. There's a football in the centre of the carriage.)*

ALICE. Hi? *I really need to talk to you, and no-one's been any help, and –*

*(**DEE** nods excitedly to the football.)*

You want me to... what kick the...?

No. No. I want to *talk* to you.

*(**ALICE** kicks the ball. They're both delighted and cheer.)*

Great! So, now. Help me.

Hello? Do you guys just stare at the ball all day?

(But they're focussed on the ball again.)

Oh my god.

*(**ALICE** opens her backpack, takes out a compass from her bag, and punctures the ball.)*

DEE. I knew that was going to happen.

ALICE. Well – well – TALK TO / ME THEN –

DUM. *(To **DUM**.)* No you didn't.

ALICE. Didn't what?

DEE. I would have put money on it.

ALICE. Money?

DUM. Oh yeah?

DEE. Yeah.

DUM. Well I would have put money on it too.

DEE. *Well I would have put more.*

DUM. How much more?

DEE. 85p!

DUM. 85p more or just 85p!

DEE. *(Fury in his eyes.)* OH *YEAH, YOU'D LIKE TO KNOW THAT WOULDN'T YOU.*

DUM. *YEAH I WOULD.*

DEE. *(Fury in his eyes.)* OH *YEAH, YOU'D LOVE TO KNOW THAT WOULDN'T YOU.*

DUM. *YEAH I WOULD.*

ALICE. Excuse me.

BOTH. WHAT.

ALICE. I just want to get off the train. I'm going to my Nani's house.

(They both laugh.)

DUM. You're joking.

DEE. No she's not.

DUM. She is. She's chatting absolute Chorleywood!

DEE. SHE'S NOT.

DUM. She is, I bet she doesn't even want to go!

DEE. No she's not I bet she does!

DUM. Yes she is I bet she doesn't!

DEE. No she's not I bet she does!

(They're locking eyes again, fuming.)

ALICE. Well I don't actually *want* to go to Nani's – she makes us sit at the table and tells us long stories and then forgets she's told them and tells them all over again.

DEE. So you don't wanna go?

ALICE. No!

DUM. HAHA. / SCOOOOOOOOOORE!

(Orange light spins through the carriage again. A few sparks fly. Meow.)

OI GET OFF THE PITCH.

DEE. I could Kilburn that cat.

BOTH. Oi!

(The orange light disappears. **ALICE** *makes for the door.)*

DUM. *(To* **ALICE***.)* You need to stop changing carriages.

DEE. Or the Queen's gonna throw you in the Gap.

BOTH. Oooooh!

DEE. And anyway – we're going exactly where we need to go –

ALICE. Where's that?

BOTH. *(Excited.) To the footy!*

DUM. It's the one thing we agree on.

BOTH. Oi!

DEE. I'm going to the Arsenal at Cannons Park.

ALICE. That's not where Arsenal is –

DUM. I've heard they've got great grass at Green Park.

DEE. I want to see the little team at Belsize Park.

DUM. She's probably just taking us to Queen's Park.

ALICE. Why don't you just go to Wembley Park?

DUM. Don't be a nosey Parker.

BOTH. Oi!

DEE. Play a game with us, pass the time.

ALICE. I'm so bad at football the teacher lets me play chess in the changing rooms. Oi!

DUM. This one is a bit of a *Sloane Square*.

BOTH. Oi!

ALICE. Why don't you just play together?

DUM. You're not gonna catch us running about the pitch!

ALICE. …why not?

BOTH. WE PLAY IN GOAL.

*(**ALICE** makes for the door again. **DEE** rushes over and blocks the door.)*

ALICE. Get out my way!

BOTH. You're not leaving!

*(**ALICE** has an idea.)*

ALICE. I'll play both of you on *one condition*.

DEE. YESSSS!

DUM. What's the condition?

ALICE. You have to be on the same team. Bet you can't do that.

*(**DUM** and **DEE** lock eyes.)*

DUM. 85p says we can do it.

DEE. 85p says we can't.

DUM. Can.

DEE. Can't.

DUM. CAN.

DEE. CAN'T.

DUM. CAN.

DEE. CAN'T.

DUM. CAN – I'M NOTORIOUSLY A GREAT TEAM PLAYER

DEE. NO YOU'RE NOT

DUM. I'M GONNA AGREE WITH EVERYTHING YOU SAY

DEE. I'VE HAD ENOUGH OF YOUR TOTTERIDGE.

DUM. I WILL, I WILL

DEE. YOU / WON'T

DUM. I BLUMMIN WOULD, / I BLUMMIN WOULD, WE'LL BE PLAYING THE SAME TEAM BEFORE YOU BLUMMIN KNOW IT

DEE. THE LAST THING I'D EVER DO IS AGREE WITH YOU, YOU ARE SO THICK, YOU'RE THICKER THAN THICKNESS

> (*They're up in each other's faces. Shouting.* **ALICE** *slowly walks around them.*)

ALICE. Guys!

BOTH. What?

ALICE. OPEN GOAL.

BOTH. No, wait, no!

> (**ALICE** *runs through the door, and shuts it behind her.*)

AWWWWWW.

Five

> (**ALICE** *emerges into a fairly regular looking carriage. Commuters all over, on phones.*)
>
> (*She sits and takes deep breaths.*)

ALICE. (*to herself.*) I feel like I'm losing my mind. Everything's gonna be fine. Though I'm in doubt, I'll figure it out. There's got to be some sort of sign.

> (*She sits, gets out her phone, rings someone. It doesn't go through.*)

Agh.

> (*She opens a messenger app and holds record.*)

Hi. Mum. I haven't got any signal. So, I'm leaving this in case it sends. I'm on the train, but it's not a normal train – and – there was a rabbit, and these two goalies – and I don't know how to get back – and, and. You always said if you're feeling scared I should just take a deep breath and go through my rhymes but I've been doing it but it's not working and – Has something happened? Did I do something wrong? Have I disappeared? Mum. I miss you. I'm… I'm… [scared]

> (**ALICE** *stares at the phone.*)

… Delete…

Hi Mum. I haven't got any signal. So I'm leaving this in case it sends. This is to say I'm fine. I know where I'm going. I'll see you at Nani's.

> (*The tannoy squeaks again:*)

QUEEN. Good evening Passengers! I have some *bad news*. Black as Burnt Oak. Graver than Highgate. It seems we have an *Overgrounder* on the train.

> *(The Commuters slowly turn to look at* **ALICE**.*)*

ALICE. Haha. Hi. Who's she... who's she talking about?

QUEEN. So, I'm afraid to say I've had to release the Jabberwocky. In fact it's on its way to you right now. And Overgrounder... if you're listening, which I'm sure you are. Give yourself up now. It's going to make this easier for everyone.

> *(Screeeech.)*
>
> *(Then, again. Screeeeeeeech.)*
>
> *(The lights begin to flicker out.)*
>
> *(Louder. Screeeeeeeeeeeeech.)*
>
> *(The carriage is plunged into darkness. The Commuters disappear. We see glimpses: a gigantic, curling claw constructed from wires and rail tracks. A long tail. A huge, blinking eye.)*
>
> *(**ALICE** hides under a seat. She makes herself as small as she can. The screeching becomes louder. Its breath fogs up the carriage. It nears **ALICE**... she stays quiet.)*
>
> *(An orange light appears. It jumps around.)*

ALICE. No. Cat. Go away. No.

> *(It jumps down into her phone.)*

PHONE. *Meow.*

ALICE. SHHH!

(Jabberwocky lunges at her.)

*(**ALICE** scrambles up, and heads for the door.)*

*(**ALICE** sprints from carriage to carriage, passing Commuters, dodging the claws of the Jabberwocky. The further away she gets, the bigger it seems.)*

Six

(A cosy carriage, made up like a kitchen. The **TORTOISE** *is preparing to cook. A cardigan, and a huge backpack.* **ALICE** *barrels in terrified.)*

ALICE. There's a monster – it had huge claws and jaws and *roars* – oh my god I don't know what it was but it was *creepy* and it was going to eat me – and the more I ran away the bigger it got.

TORTOISE. Well, the more you run away from problems, the *bigger they get*. Sounds like you just met the Jabberwocky?

ALICE. Jabberwhatty?

TORTOISE. Jabber*wocky*.

You know... the jaws that bite, the claws that catch...

*(***ALICE*** is pinching herself absentmindedly.)*

Relax. Sit down. Kettle's on. Hungry?

ALICE. I'm alright thanks.

TORTOISE. If I had known you were coming I've bought more Swiss Cottage Cheese. Russel you up a Square meal. Where've you been?

ALICE. Well I've been –

TORTOISE. Beans?

*(***TORTOISE*** takes out a can that reads: EAT ME.)*

ALICE. Eat me...

Wait. Wait wait wait wait wait. I know who you are!

TORTOISE. You do?

(**ALICE** *scrambles through her backpack and pulls out the book,* Alice in Wonderland.*)*

ALICE. This is from the book. You're all from the book. I'm so – AGH! – I'm so *stupid*. There's Rabbit and Tweedle Dee and Tweedle Dum, there's a cat floating about – and you're the… the… *(Flicking through the book.)* MOCK TURTLE!

TORTOISE. *(Offended.)* A turtle?! I'm a tortoise, not a turtle. *I've got hands not flippers.*

ALICE. *(Still reading.)* Have you seen a caterpillar?

TORTOISE. A Caterpillar, *I don't think so!*

ALICE. *(Shouting at the book.)* What is going on?

TORTOISE. Calm yourself. It's coming up and we're going to watch.

ALICE. Watch?

TORTOISE. I better watch my watch, or we'll miss it!

ALICE. Watch what?

TORTOISE. Watch what's whiling away out the window. This train chugs through the deep subconscious of the city. Every six hours on the dot, we pass a pool of hopes and dreams. It's beautiful, you *have* to see it.

I used to be like you – Kings Crossing around… through the Southgates, over the Archways, getting into trouble in every carriage, escaping by the skin of my shell…

ALICE. I thought the Queen doesn't let anyone out of their carriage?

TORTOISE. The Queen wasn't always in charge.

ALICE. Who was in charge?

TORTOISE. Oh you haven't met her yet? She was *chaos*. Fun, but *chaos*.

(She strokes a seat.)

ALICE. What are you doing?

TORTOISE. She likes being petted.

ALICE. The train?

TORTOISE. She's a good girl.

ALICE. You're so weird.

TORTOISE. Why be normal? Give me a bit of excitement then. Where are you from?

ALICE. …Brixton.

TORTOISE. Brixton. What a lovely word. Tell me about *Brixton*.

ALICE. Er. *I don't know.*

TORTOISE. What does it make you think of?

ALICE. *Busy.*

TORTOISE. Hustling and bustling?

ALICE. Yeah – people, so many people, all the time.

TORTOISE. What else?

ALICE. There's a park. And there's a swimming pool. But it's not a swimming pool. It's called a… a… a Lido.

TORTOISE. A LIDO!

ALICE. Why are you so excited?

TORTOISE. It's been so long since I've heard about something *new*.

ALICE. There's – um – the Ritzy –

TORTOISE. Is that a fancy hotel!?

ALICE. No, it's a cinema. And there's a market.

TORTOISE. What do they sell?

ALICE. Food from all around the world.

TORTOISE. And where is this market?

ALICE. Electric Avenue.

TORTOISE. ELECTRIC AVENUE!? THAT SOUNDS … ELECTRIC!

ALICE. …what?

TORTOISE. I'm imagining all the vegetables lighting up like lightbulbs! I'd go but… who would water my tree?

ALICE. Me and Mum go a lot – she's been taking me on these… she calls them adventures. Ever since –

TORTOISE. Since what?

ALICE. Mum and Dad split up. It's a good thing, they're much happier but – well – recently she's been… different. Weird.

TORTOISE. Weird like I'm weird? Or weird like… *weird.*

ALICE. She changed jobs – she used to write jingles for businesses in Brixton –

TORTOISE. An artist!

ALICE. It was so fun, she met all these cool people, they played all her stuff on Brixton Radio. Every day was different, sometimes she would take me to a party and we'd come back at midnight! I'd be so tired the next day, but she would be up in the recording studio – we have this little storage cupboard we turned into a recording studio. But this new job – it's like this whole other part of her has switched off. It's like she's a different person. Last week she was in the recording room and I heard her –

TORTOISE. Heard her what?

ALICE. Nothing.

TORTOISE. *You know, when I was your age –*

(**ALICE** *huffs.*)

What?

ALICE. That is the beginning of every one of my Nani's boring stories.

TORTOISE. Oh.

ALICE. No. Sorry. Tell me.

TORTOISE. *When I was your age*, a little girl won me at a funfair. She also won a giant fluffy Pikachu. Took us both home on the tube, and who got forgotten on the seat? Not the Pikachu, I'll tell you that for free! Life – it's like Hyde Park, it's got Corners! Do you write these... jingles too?

ALICE. I write bars at break and lunch. They're like jingles but better.

TORTOISE. Can I hear one?

ALICE. No. They're for me.

(Beat. A timer goes off.)

TORTOISE. There it is!

(Blue lights start to shimmer through the window.)

ALICE. Wow...

TORTOISE. The pool of hopes and dreams. Where the imaginations of the population bubbles away. Look at them gyring and gimbling up to the surface! Look how *alive* they are.

(They watch for a while. It enchants them.)

ALICE. Not many of them though.

TORTOISE. That's because – you see that darkness? That's fear. Fear can eat everything up.

(The dreams are gone.)

I wouldn't normally show anyone this, but...

*(**TORTOISE** reveals a sword, glowing purple and orange and red.)*

ALICE. WOAH. What is that?

TORTOISE. This is the *vorpal sword*. Found it years ago stuffed behind a seat.

Me and this sword, we did everything together.

ALICE. Can I have it?!

TORTOISE. Of course you can't. She's dangerous. I pray to the Seven Sisters I never need to use her again. I've since found there's always other ways.

ALICE. If I went to the Queen with this and *battled her* do you think she'd let me off.

TORTOISE. I wouldn't Bank on it.

ALICE. How else am I going to get to Nani's.

TORTOISE. I thought you didn't want to see her.

ALICE. Maybe she has some good stories. Like you. Do you want to come with me?

TORTOISE. We've all got to Mind the Gap between our heads and our necks with the Queen in charge.

ALICE. Don't tell me you're scared of the Queen too.

TORTOISE. She says she's taking us exactly where we need to go.

ALICE. We need to do something about this Queen!

TORTOISE. If she hears you, you're in deep Bayswater...

ALICE. I don't care if she hears me! She's making everyone miserable. You need to get out of here. Look. Will you help me or not?

TORTOISE. Ach. Fine. You didn't hear this from me. But... *(Whispers.)* find *the Tea Party*.

ALICE. *The Tea Party.*

TORTOISE. Yes. And remember. *Krapy Rubsnif.*

ALICE. *Krapy Rubsnif?*

TORTOISE. *Krapy Rubsnif*!

ALICE. What does that mean?

TORTOISE. Things aren't always *straight forward*. You'll know when you know.

ALICE. Thank you.

TORTOISE. Thank *you*. Oh and –

ALICE. Mind the Gap. Got it.

TORTOISE. Good Girl.

Seven

*(**ALICE** steps through an empty carriage, full of determination. She recites to herself:)*

ALICE.
I'M NOT LOSING MY MIND.
EVERYTHING'S GONNA BE FINE.
THINGS AREN'T AS BAD AS THEY SEEM.
I'LL GET OFF THE TRAIN.
ONCE I TACKLE THE QUEEN...

(The tannoy screeches:)

QUEEN. I'm afraid to say the Overgrounder has not yet been located.

(She freezes.)

*(On the LED screen, a **CAT**'s eyes appear.)*

Which means I'm going to have to Acton this with severe measures.

MEOW.

Sorry about that. I'm going to have to – *MEOW*

That Cat is in the tannoy again! DISTRICT!

DISTRICT. Yes Mam?

QUEEN. Sort this out right now. I need you to delete this irritating creature from the system!

*(Tannoy cuts out. **ALICE** looks at the **CAT**.)*

ALICE. You did that didn't you.

CAT. Yes. Ehehehehe.

*(The **CAT** disappears, and appears behind her. Meow.)*

(**ALICE** *spins again, the* **CAT** *disappears.*)

ALICE. Where are you?

(**ALICE**'s *phone buzzes. The* **CAT** *is on her phone.*)

CAT. Everywhere.

(**ALICE** *throws her phone away, it slides across the floor.*)

(*Oooh. Messages.*)

ALICE. Get out of my phone.

CAT. Ticklish in here.

ALICE. Get off my messages.

CAT. Ignoring your Mother?

ALICE. She messages me all the time, which one am I meant to reply to?

CAT. Hm. Not many contacts. Not very Poplar are you?

What's this? Rhymes in the notes app.

ALICE. Don't look at those! They're rubbish.

CAT.
"WHEN YOU WALK INTO THE ROOM
HARRY STYLES YOU MAKE MY HEART GO BOOM?"

ALICE. OKAY. Shut up! Stop! Cheshire Cat get out –

CAT. I'm NOT THE CHESHIRE CAT!

I'm the Chesham cat… hehehehehe –

ALICE. I'm deleting you.

CAT. Oooh the girls' group chat from school!

ALICE. What do you –

CAT. Oops – sorry – you're not in that chat are you.

ALICE. What are they saying?

CAT. Wouldn't you like to know.

ALICE. You're chatting – what is it – you're chatting absolute Chorleywood.

CAT. Oh get off your Highbury horse hehehehehe.

ALICE. GET OUT. GET OUT OF MY PHONE.

CAT. Alright. You don't have to shout. It really is a shame, isn't it. I thought you could help me get the truth out there... But turns out you're just like everyone else here – you're stuck...

ALICE. You're stuck? – What are you talking about? Hello?

*(But the **CAT** is gone.)*

*(Mimicking **CAT**.)* You don't *know* me. Come on Alice. Tea Party.

(She steps through.)

Eight

(This carriage is old school Alice in Wonderland. *A tea party in the centre of the carriage.)*

*(***NOSE***,* **PIGEON***, and* **RAT** *are there, laying the table, dressed in Victorian clothes.)*

(The **PIGEON** *spins around, very nervous, affecting an old fashioned accent:)*

PIGEON. Oh. OH. Welcome to the er – to the *Tea Party*. Some – some tea? Perhaps madam would like some tea!

*(***PIGEON** *grabs teabags and offers them out.)*

RAT. *(Also doing posh voice, even shakier.)* WHAT ABOUT SOME *BISCUITS???*

(The **RAT** *offers a cake stand, full of biscuits, but she's shaking.)*

(The **NOSE** *turns around. His entire head is a nose.* **ALICE** *stares at him in astonishment. Then the* **NOSE** *takes a vial from his belt, and sprays it in her face.)*

ALICE. *Lavender?*

PIGEON. The weather is! Gosh! The weather *is* today isn't it.

RAT. It is!

PIGEON. It really is. Have you met my friend the esteemed Nose?

(The **NOSE** *sneezes.* **RAT** *drops her voice:)*

RAT. *Shut up.*

ALICE. The Tortoise sent me. I want to get rid of the Queen.

(! – everyone is on edge.)

PIGEON. *Get rid of the Queen. We're not doing that. Why do you think we're doing that? We're just having a Tea Party!*

*(**RAT** whispers in **PIGEON**'s ear.)*

Secret Password. Right! Yeah. Yeah.

*(To **ALICE**.)* Have you – *do you happen to have the secret passwor*d?

ALICE. The password?

PIGEON. *The password that might let someone know, if they were plotting against the Queen*

PIGEON & RAT. *Which we're not.*

PIGEON. *That they were on your side...*

ALICE. Wait wait wait! I do! I do! What was it. Krapyrubsnif!

PIGEON. Oh thank God.

ALL CHANGE!

*(**PIGEON**, **RAT** and **NOSE** completely relax. Their voices change.)*

ALICE. What does it mean anyway? Krapyrubsnif?

PIGEON. It's Finsbury Park backwards.

*(**RAT**, **NOSE** and **PIGEON** take off their Victorian coats to reveal tracksuits.)*

*(**PIGEON** presses a button under the table and it flips over. It's now covered in maps and*

plans. The record scratches out, and Low-Fi beats fill the air.)

RAT. Don't drink that.

PIGEON. I hate that stuff. Welcome, I'm Pigeon.

RAT. I'm Rat.

PIGEON. And he's Nose.

*(The **NOSE** sprays a cartridge. **ALICE** smells.)*

ALICE. Peppermint?

PIGEON. Peppermint's a bit like a handshake.

RAT. Nice, dependable, not too over the top.

PIGEON. The thing about nose, is that he always sprays what he means.

RAT. We're waiting for the Chatter.

ALICE. You mean the Hatter?

PIGEON. No, the Chatter. She's the Boss.

RAT. Our Glorious Leader who will help us overthrow the Queen and regain our rightful places on the carriage, steering the steel for all eternity! Oh, how wonderful it will be when we reclaim what is rightfully ours, the sun finally rising on our band of merry adventurers –

PIGEON. Rat. You're getting carried away again.

RAT. Right. Sorry.

PIGEON. Take a seat.

ALICE. But I don't get it. None of you are from *Alice in Wonderland*.

PIGEON. What are you talking about?

*(**ALICE** shows the book.)*

ALICE. The book –

PIGEON. This is real, it's not based on a book.

ALICE. There's a rabbit, and two idiots, and a turtle – I thought next there'd be, I don't know, a caterpillar who vapes or something –

PIGEON. If it is based on a book it would be an extraordinary adaptation. Or maybe the book is based on this! Ever think about that?

RAT. Or maybe it's nothing to do with a book. Maybe we're the psycho-drama playing out inside an eleven-year old girl's mind! Maybe we are the chemicals racing round the brain of an adolescent, desperately trying to make sense of an impossible situation, filtering it through the thousand prisms of reality that make up this distracted globe –

PIGEON. Rat.

RAT. Sorry.

PIGEON. What we're trying to say is, don't pigeon-hole us.

*(**PIGEON** coos.)*

ALICE. Who are you?

PIGEON. We're the guys you never want to see on a tube.

ALICE. A pigeon, a rat, and a –?

*(**NOSE** sniffs in.)*

PIGEON. Runny nose.

(The window opens, and wind rips through the carriage.)

*(The **CHATTER** slips through. She's wearing a modified tube driver's uniform. She is played by the actor who plays Mum.)*

CHATTER. *(Off.)* MUSIC PLEASE.

PIGEON. Here we go.

> (**PIGEON**, **RAT** and **NOSE** *strike up instruments.* **NOSE** *beatboxes with* **NOSE** *sounds.)*

CHATTER. The tongue the teeth the tip of the tongue.
I AM THE MOST NONSENSICAL INCOMPREHENSIBLE
JIBBERISH SPITTER BUT STILL INCREDIBLE

ONLY THE MOST NOTORIOUS GLORIOUS CURIOUS
    SPURIOUS TALKATIVE FORCE IN ALL OF THIS
CHATTIEST BATTIEST KILLER OF CAUTION
SOME WOULD SAY I'M A SORCERESS
CONJURING FUN IN ABUNDANCE
GETTING APPLAUSE FROM THE AUDIENCE.

> *(Crowd goes wild.)*

A MIRACLE LYRICAL PUZZLING QUIZZICAL COOL
    INDIVIDUAL KEEPING THESE STUPID RULES TO A
    MINIMAL.
NOT UNORIGINAL THAT'S UNFORGIVABLE
FORMIDABLE
FIRST LADY OF THE MIC
GETTING YOU HYPE
I AM THE CHAMPION OF PATTER
KNOWN TO EVERYONE HERE AS THEEEEEEEEEE

ALL BUT ALICE. *Chatter!!!*

ALICE. *Mum...?!*

CHATTER. Who the bloomin' Bakerloo is this?

ALICE. I'm... Alice?

CHATTER. I can't hear her.

ALICE. I'm Alice!

CHATTER. I said I can't hear her.

PIGEON. *(Whispered.)* She wants you to rap it back, you know rap music?

ALICE. No.

CHATTER. What! You don't spit?

ALICE. I do but. They're not for anyone. They're just for me. I don't *perform*.

PIGEON. Do it. Trust me.

>*(**PIGEON** plays some beats on a keyboard, and **NOSE** beatboxes.)*

ALICE. *(Tentatively.)* ALICE-TOCRACY, ALICE-STOCRACY,
I'M THE QUEEN OF THE SOUND NO-ONES STOPPIN' ME.
ALICE-TOCRACY, ALICE-STOCRACY,
I'M THE BEST AND THERE'S NO MEDIOCRITY.

CHATTER. No no no. She can't join my revolution if she can't Turnham Green with envy.

>*(**PIGEON** and **NOSE** pick **ALICE** up to take her out.)*

ALICE. Revolution?

CHATTER. I used to drive this train. I used to be on that mic. Bringing a bit of brightness to everyone's day. We're getting me back where I belong.

ALICE. All I want is the Queen to let me off.

CHATTER. She'll never let you...

>*(**ALICE** is pulled toward the door.)*

...but, *I* might. *IF I knew your name.*

ALICE. Fine. FINE! Let me go again.

>*(Oooohs from **PIGEON**, sprays from **NOSE**.)*

CHATTER. One more shot. Hopefully this time you can find the right flow. Let's go.

ALICE.
>I'M ALICE, I'M ALICE, GREEN PARK FOR BUCKINGHAM PALACE
>YEAH!
>I'M ALICE, I'M ALICE GREEN PARK FOR BUCKINGHAM PALACE
>
>ALICE-TOCRACY, ALICE-TOCRACY
>I'M THE QUEEN OF THE SOUND NOTHINGS STOPPING ME
>ALICE-TOCRACY, ALICE-TOCRACY
>I'M THE BEST AND THERE'S NO MEDIOCRITY
>
>ALICE-TOCRACY, ALICE-TOCRACY
>I'M THE QUEEN OF THE SOUND NOTHINGS STOPPING ME
>ALICE-TOCRACY, ALICE-TOCRACY
>I'M THE BEST AND THERE'S NO MEDIOCRITY
>
>EVERYONE LISTEN UP GATHER ROUND
>I AM THE BRAND NEW ACTON TOWN
>SOON I'LL BE BIGGER THAN MANOR HOUSE
>I'VE GOT MORE LINES THAN THE UNDERGROUND
>GOSPEL OAK YOU CAN'T HACKNEY DOWNS
>GOT WAY MORDEN CAMDEN TOWN
>GET ON YOUR NEASDEN YOU HAVE TO BOW
>ELIZABETH LINE? I HAVE THE CROWN!
>
>ALICE-TOCRACY, ALICE-TOCRACY
>I'M THE QUEEN OF THE SOUND NOTHINGS STOPPING ME
>ALICE-TOCRACY, ALICE-TOCRACY
>I'M THE BEST AND THERE'S NO MEDIOCRITY!

>*(Cheers!)*

CHATTER. Girl. You're in.

ALICE. Let's go then. The Tortoise she has a sword – we'll get it– we'll battle –

CHATTER. Hold on. Hold on.

PIGEON. We can't just barge in to the throne room.

CHATTER. ALL CHANGE.

> *(Everyone gets up and changes seat.)*

PIGEON. Meeting number three-hundred-and-twenty-six of the Revolting Revolution.

RAT. The Queen has stolen Boss's spot in the driver's seat, and we're going to boot her.

ALICE. Great! So, I was thinking –

CHATTER. ALL CHANGE.

ALICE. Oh *no*.

> *(**CHATTER**, **PIGEON**, **NOSE** and **RAT** dig into their pockets, and drop small change onto the table.)*

CHATTER. About 85p all in all.

RAT. Right, does anyone want a coffee? Flat White-City? Tooting Becspresso?

ALICE. No! Focus. We need to boot her.

PIGEON. Boot who?

ALICE. *The Queen.*

CHATTER. We've got plans.

ALICE. What are they?

CHATTER. Very well. Nose?

> *(**NOSE** places a huge stack of papers on the table. **PIGEON** and **RAT** start up the music.)*

If you want to get off the train

There's only one way.

That is *down with the Queen.*

Hahaha.

If I get back on the driver's seat, I'll take you to Brixton, now, repeat after me.

DOWN WITH THE QUEEN!
YOU KNOW WHAT TO DO
DOWN WITH THE QUEEN
I'M TALKING TO YOU
DOWN WITH THE QUEEN
FRONT ROW, BACK ROW
DOWN WITH THE QUEEN
LEFT AND RIGHT
DOWN WITH THE QUEEN!
ONE MORE TIME
DOWN WITH THE QUEEN!
IF YOU WANT TO GET OFF THE TRAIN
THERE'S ONLY WAY THAT'S DOWN WITH THE QUEEN.

ALICE. Who are you talking to?

CHATTER.

WE'LL DISTRACT THE QUEEN ONCE I'M IN THE CHAIR I'LL LET YOU OFF DOES THAT SOUND FAIR?

TIME TO ACT EVERYONE PREPARE

I COULD CATCH HER OUT WHILE SHE'S UNAWARE

AND MAKE A BLINDFOLD OUT OF HER UNDERWEAR

PLAYING ENDLESS CHESS WITH A HUNDRED SQUARES

OR ENDLESS SNAP

FOREVER TRAPPED

DUE THE FACT SHE HASN'T GOT A PAIR

ANOTHER WAY OF TAKING HER DOWN?

MECHANICAL LEGS AT THE BASE OF HER CROWN

SPENDING ALL HER DAYS TRYNA CHASE IT AROUND

HMMM? WHAT OTHER WAYS HAVE FOUND?

LURE HER OUT WITH A CHEEKY KEBAB

SHE'LL OPEN THE BOOTH GREETED BY FANS

WHILE YOU PRETEND TO ASK FOR A SELFIE
I'LL SNEAK UP TO THE SEAT ALL STEALTHY.

DOWN WITH THE QUEEN
YOU KNOW WHAT TO DO
DOWN WITH THE QUEEN
I'M TALKING TO YOU
DOWN WITH THE QUEEN
FRONT ROW, BACK ROW
DOWN WITH THE QUEEN
LEFT AND RIGHT
DOWN WITH THE QUEEN!
ONE MORE TIME
DOWN WITH THE QUEEN!

IF YOU WANNA GET OFF THIS TRAIN THERE'S ONLY ONE WAY THAT'S
DOWN WITH THE QUEEN

TAKE DOWN THE QUEEN I'M ON IT!
WE'LL FILL HER CUP OF TEA WITH SCOTCH BONNETS
SHE'LL RUN OUTSIDE LOOKING FOR MILK
AND I'LL HOP UP IN THE BOOTH AND LOCK IT
MAKE HER LOOK AT HER FACE IN THE MIRROR
AND SHE'LL RUN AS FAR AS ALDGATE TO PINNER
LEAVE IT TO US, SHE'LL LEAVE IN DISGUST
ONCE SHE DISCOVERS THERE'S HAIR IN HER DINNER.

HMM WHAT OTHER THINGS CAN WE DO?
CREEPY CRAWLIES INTO HER SHOES
MAKE HER JUMP WHEN I SURPRISE HER
SNEAK UP BEHIND HER AND SAY BOO.
I'LL BE DRIVING THE TRAIN IN AN INSTANT
MAKING ANNOUNCEMENTS, CHANGING THE RHYTHM
DOWN WITH THE QUEEN LETS GO THE FULL DISTANCE
DON'T WORRY ALICE I'LL GET YOU TO BRIXTON.

DOWN WITH THE QUEEN!
REPEAT AFTER ME

DOWN WITH THE QUEEN!
1,2,3
DOWN WITH THE QUEEN!
LEFT AND RIGHT
DOWN WITH THE QUEEN!
FRONT ROW, BACK ROW
DOWN WITH THE QUEEN
ONE MORE TIME
DOWN WITH THE QUEEN!

IF YOU WANNA GET OFF THIS TRAIN THERE'S ONLY ONE WAY THAT'S
DOWN WITH THE QUEEN!

ALICE. They all sound GREAT! Let's go!

CHATTER. Hold on hold on. I've just had another idea.

(**CHATTER** *starts scribbling.*)

ALICE. But –

CHATTER. Shh.

ALICE. Just pick one –

RAT. Don't interrupt, we're working.

(*Pause. They're all scribbling away.*)

ALICE. How many plans have you made?

PIGEON. Seven hundred and twenty three.

ALICE. And how many have you – actually – *done*.

CHATTER. Give me TIME. I've got to find the perfect one.

ALICE. So you just sit here?

CHATTER. Come and join us. It's fun!

ALICE. I don't care if it's fun! You're not helping anything. You're just letting her win!

CHATTER. I'm leading this revolution. Not you.

ALICE. So, how long are we going to be here? We're just going to sit around drinking tea, nothing happening – We've got to move forward!

CHATTER. Right. I'm at my Mile End with this.

*(**CHATTER** storms off.)*

ALICE. Chatter, wait –

PIGEON. Wait boss – wait.

She's gone again.

(But she's gone.)

RAT. To answer your question. We have enacted precisely zero of those plans.

*(The **NOSE** sprays. **ALICE** smells.)*

ALICE. Nani's House? Why spray that?

*(**RAT NOSE** and **PIGEON** leave.)*

Wait, wait, how do I stop the Queen?

PIGEON. I don't know. Maybe the answer's in your blummin book.

(They're gone.)

ALICE. The book. The ending. The ending. How does she get out?

*(**ALICE** flicks through the book, and reads from it.)*

The Queen's about to cut her head off, and Alice… Alice… here. The queen and all of the soldiers surround her and she *shouts at the top of her voice "You're nothing but a pack of cards."*

And then they all turn into cards. And then she wakes up.

Okay. If all else fails, just say something like that. I'll just say… you're nothing but a… stupid tube map. Yeah. You're nothing but a stupid tube map.

Nine

(**ALICE** *lands in another carriage. A large, long throne room. Two* **GUARDS** *march in.* **CIRCLE** *and* **DISTRICT**.)

BOTH. NORTHOLT!

(*They stop.*)

ALICE. Here to speak to the Queen.

CIRCLE. Have a booking?

DISTRICT. You'll need a booking.

CIRCLE. If you don't have a booking you can't get a looking.

ALICE. Well then let me make a booking.

DISTRICT. You can't do a booking here you do it in the app.

ALICE. Hello? Queen?

CIRCLE. Shhhhh.

ALICE. Queen! Please!

DISTRICT. There are rules. There are regulations.

CIRCLE. *Directions of travel.*

DISTRICT. Hammersmith! Hammersmith! We have a problem.

(**HAMMERSMITH** *thuds in. An enforcer with a gigantic pink hammer.*)

HAMMERS. Show. Me. Problem.

(**HAMMERSMITH** *narrows in on* **ALICE**.)

ALICE. It's just I'd… I'd really like to… um… um… er…

(The door at the other end of the carriage is thrown open. A long carpet, made of tube seat material, rolls out.)

*(The **QUEEN OF THE LINE** enters on a throne. The **LINES** all kneel.)*

*(The **QUEEN OF THE LINE** is played by the same actor who plays Mum.)*

QUEEN. Why didn't you tell me she was here?

CIRCLE. Well – um. Ma'am. We were just – just –

QUEEN. What? Speak clearly.

CIRCLE & DISTRICT. We were – um…we got our –

Got our lines crossed.

QUEEN. Sounds like a signal failure – do you need some *maintenance*!?

CIRCLE & DISTRICT. No ma'am sorry ma'am.

QUEEN. I'm sorry I was just dealing with something. A bit of a Snaresbrook in our system.

(Meow.)

ALICE. Are you the Queen then?

*(The **LINES** also laugh.)*

QUEEN. Ha. Hahahahaha.

ALICE. You look like the – just like the – [Chatter]

QUEEN. Look at you, Common as Clapham. How can I help?

ALICE. I want you to stop the train and let me get off.

QUEEN. Stop the train? Ha. Hahahahaha.

ALICE. Stop laughing…

QUEEN. You don't get a say in this. I'm a Royal Oak and you are a ghastly little Shepherd's Bush. I'm not letting you off.

ALICE. Why not?

QUEEN. Why not? She's asking me why not! *Because I said so.*

ALICE. Then where are we going?

QUEEN. Wouldn't you like to know.

ALICE. And when are you getting there?

QUEEN. Honestly, no-one needs the answer to these trivial little questions –

ALICE. They do! These are *basic!*

QUEEN. If you think I came all the way out here, leaving the drivers' seat unattended, to be shouted at by a little girl –

ALICE. I'm not trying to I'm – I'm just – I'm – I'm trying to –

QUEEN. Come on. *Use your English.*

ALICE. Oh my god shut up.

QUEEN. Wow! I thought we were having a *conversation*. It seems like you just want to argue.

ALICE. *(It bursts out.)* You're making all their lives miserable. Why can't anyone talk to each other?!

QUEEN. Because we DON'T TALK TO EACH OTHER ON THE TUBE.

ALICE. Let the Chatter drive.

QUEEN. The Chatter! Are you joking! When she drove the train it was a nightmare. Turbulence. Changing tracks. Once she even steered the train through a rail-storm and came out the other end with a Jabberwocky. It was *me* who had to tame it!

ALICE. Please. I've got to get back. My Mum's probably worried.

QUEEN. Ohhh Mummy's worried. Wahhhh.

ALICE. AND I SHOUTED AT HER AND I FEEL GUILTY OKAY? AND I PROBABLY SHOULD SAY SORRY –

QUEEN. Alice, I'm trying to meet you halfway, but you're crying like a baby, so I don't want to talk to you anymore.

ALICE. I don't want to talk to you!

QUEEN. What do you want to do, then?

ALICE. *Ugh! I want to – I want to – throw you off the train!*

QUEEN. Right well that's a threat, isn't it. Guards. Pinner.

(The **LINES** *leap up and grab* **ALICE**.*)*

ALICE. The book – the book –

*(***ALICE** *desperately reads from the book, then closes her eyes tight.)*

You are *nothing, nothing* but a stupid tube map!

(Beat.)

Nothing but a stupid tube map!

Nothing but a...

A ...

QUEEN. What you talking about now?

ALICE. I'm meant to wake up now.

QUEEN. The book?

*(**HAMMERSMITH** grunts and snatches **ALICE**'s book and hands it to the **QUEEN**.)*

She thinks this is based on a book. Ha. Hahahahaha.

God *this* Queen is useless!

*(The **QUEEN** tears the book in half, and pages fly everywhere.)*

ALICE. Let me go!

QUEEN. No no no! You're a serious danger to the train.

ALICE. *I hate you.*

QUEEN. Throw her in the Gap.

ALICE. No – *NO.*

(One of the guards opens the train door. The Gap stretches out before us. A silent and mysterious portal – a dream space.)

Let me go! LET ME GO.

It's not a dream is it.

QUEEN. No dear. No it's not.

*(**ALICE** enters the Gap. The stage snaps to black.)*

(Meow.)

ACT TWO

One

(Absence. Total darkness. A hole that swallows us up.)

(All we can hear is the whistling of wind through a tunnel.)

(And then... slowly... **ALICE** *wills herself back into existence.)*

(There she is. Standing in the nothing.)

ALICE. Oh no.

Hello? Hello? *HELLO? HELP.*

HELP! ANYONE?

(It echoes. **ALICE** *sits in despair.)*

I FEEL LIKE I'M LOSING MY MIND.
STILL EVERYTHING'S GONNA BE FINE.
THINGS'LL GET BETTER IN TIME.

Why can't I think of a rhyme...

Why can't I think of a rhyme...

I need to – hello? Hello? Please? Someone? ANYONE!

(A door appears. A crack open... there's something terrifying behind it.)

(*Soundscape:*)

GIRL 1. Oh my god don't talk to her don't talk to her.

GIRL 2. She is *so weird.*

(**ALICE** *gets sniggered at and ignored.*)

LISTENER 1. This song is *so bad.*

LISTENER 2. What is she, like eleven years old?

LISTENER 1. (*Making fun.*)
ALICE-STOCRACY, ALICE-STOCRACY

LISTENER 2. That tune is *dead.*

(*They snigger.*)

ALICE. No. STOP.

(*The door appears again. Someone is crying behind the door.* **ALICE** *summons up the courage.*)

(*She approaches the door slowly. She opens it.*)

Mum...

What's wrong. Are you okay?

(*The crying gets louder and louder.*)

MUM! ARE YOU OKAY?

MUM. (*Monstrous, from behind the door.*) GO AWAY.

(**ALICE** *slams the door and cries. All is lost. She'll be here forever.*)

(*She's crying on the ground.*)

ALICE. I'm sorry – I'm sorry – I didn't mean to –

(*Then faintly, the sound of a train above.*)

(*The* **CAT** – *a physical presence, a lonely hacker in a hoodie, lowers himself down on a rope. He reaches out a hand.*)

CAT. Alice!

ALICE. Go away!

CAT. I'm... here to help.

ALICE. What? Who are you?

CAT. It's me! It's Cat!

I'm pressing save! Grab my hand!

(**ALICE** *grabs* **CAT**'s *hand.*)

Two

*(We are in **CAT**'s carriage – full of computers.)*

ALICE. You're Cat? I thought you were an app.

CAT. I'm a person! *An app!* What a stupid idea!

Sorry. Not done this much before. Meeting people. I.R.L.

Anyway, Alice –

ALICE. You shouldn't go looking through other people's phones!

CAT. I needed to see if you could be trusted –

ALICE. Are we at the back of the train?

CAT. Look. Alice –

ALICE. I thought it was haunted?

CAT. I just put up spooky gifs to keep the Queen out. But –

ALICE. I saw the train leave me behind. How did you – how did you –

CAT. This is what I'm trying to tell you if you'd just stop for a minute! The train isn't going anywhere.

ALICE. What do you mean?

CAT. The Queen says we're going where we need to go. But it's not true. I've done the maths, and... Alice. We're going in a LOOP.

ALICE. *A loop?!*

CAT. An endless circle. The Queen's been –

ALICE. She's been lying to everyone.

CAT. Yes! And the longer you stay on the train, the more likely you are to lose hope – and – and – Alice I want you to take a deep breath – you've been gone a *long time.*

ALICE. No. *No. It felt like ten minutes.*

CAT. The Gap does that. Time's not stable down there. And. I need you to take a deep breath Alice. Everyone on the train is becoming Commuters.

ALICE. What?

CAT. Rabbit, Tortoise, Dee and Dum, The Chatter's Gang – all of them. They've all lost hope.

ALICE. Well – we – we need to stop this. We need to stop *her!* Can I wake them up? Can I undo it?

CAT. I don't know.

ALICE. We've got to find Chatter. Is she –

CAT. She's off my radar entirely.

ALICE. It doesn't matter, there's no time, we have to help them.

CAT. Um...

(**ALICE** *moves to the door.*)

Alice – wait.

ALICE. What?

CAT. I can't go.

ALICE. Why not.

CAT. Because I *can't*, Okay? I can't.

ALICE. ...you're scared.

(**CAT** *nods his head.*)

Of what?

CAT. It's just... what if they hate me.

ALICE. They – they won't. Well, actually, they find you *annoying*, but –

CAT. Exactly! And if they meet me, the *me me*, what if it's even worse.

ALICE. I know how you feel. I feel that way at school. There are these girls – I worry about what they think, but – this is different people are in trouble – we have to be brave.

CAT. I'm not doing it.

ALICE. You've let that worry get too big in your head.

CAT. I'll help you from here. But that's all I can do.

(**CAT** *shakes his head. He's visibly upset.*)

ALICE. Okay. Help me from here.

(**ALICE** *is about to go, then lingers.*)

Cat. What's in the Gap?

CAT. It's the... well it's the darkness. It's –

ALICE. Where all the fears are?

CAT. Yes. Did you see something?

ALICE. Last week I saw Mum crying in her recording studio. And she shouted at me. And we haven't talked about it at all since. It was like it was happening all over again.

CAT. Oh. Alice.

ALICE. It doesn't matter. There's no time.

Three

ALICE. Chatter! Chatter! Where are you?

(The tube tannoy screeches.)

QUEEN. Good evening one and all! Still on the train, still heading exactly where we need to go. I must say these past few weeks you have really been behaving yourselves. A big well done from me.

Have a lovely night, and remember, we're right on track.

RABBIT.
WE'RE RIGHT ON TRACK.

*(**RABBIT** is revealed, typing away, he's become a Commuter.)*

ALICE. Rabbit. No no no. Rabbit. Wake up. Wake up.

RABBIT. Late… so late… so late.

*(And there's **DUM** and **DEE**. **DEE** is a Commuter. **DUM**'s arguing with her, getting no reply.)*

DUM. Why are you like this. You're always like this.

Oh yes you *are* – you are always like this.

Don't argue with me!

ALICE. Dum.

DUM. Alice. You've got to help! I think something's wrong with Dee.

ALICE. Stay there Dee, you'll be alright.

DUM. Please Alice. Help.

*(**PIGEON** is a Commuter, sitting sipping tea.)*

ALICE. Pigeon –

PIGEON. I love tea, me.

ALICE. Pigeon, what happened to your voice? Where's Rat? Where's Nose?

> (**PIGEON** *holds up a little plastic* **RAT** *and a little plastic* **NOSE**.)

No, no no –

> (**ALICE** *finds* **TORTOISE**.)

Come on. Help me. I can take you to Brixton.

TORTOISE. No no no. Nice and safe here. I don't need to leave my shell.

ALICE. Chatter. Chatter! Where are you! I need you! Chatter!

> (**CHATTER** *is sitting, staring out the window.*)

Are you... crying?

CHATTER. We're never getting off this train.

ALICE. Don't say that.

CHATTER. I'll never get back to the driver's seat.

ALICE. Yeah well – that's because you never make any decisions. You need a plan. A bit more focus and a bit less chaos.

CHATTER. What, and turn into *her*?

ALICE. No... that's not what I –

CHATTER. Sometimes I think the only way to drive the train is to be the Queen.

ALICE. I didn't mean that. I think people should be more like you, not less. My Mum she used to be like you...

CHATTER. And how much did she get done? Did she keep you safe? Did she keep everything moving? No.

Face it. I'm chaos.

ALICE. Yeah – but – but –

CHATTER. What are you saying?

ALICE. I'm – I'm saying-uh – *that*

   *(Briefly **CHATTER** becomes just like the **QUEEN**:)*

CHATTER. Use your *English*.

ALICE. I *am – UGH*.

CHATTER. Don't get moody with me –

ALICE. I'm NOT I'm trying to say –

CHATTER. What? What are you going to say that / will make it all better, it's all useless –

ALICE. I'm not saying anything, I just mean – ARG – just leave me alone. Just STOP!

It feels like we're trapped in a loop.

   *(**CHATTER** leaves.)*

ALICE. Wait. Chatter. Wait.

   (Beat.)

ALICE. ...break the loop. It's not just the train going round in circles. Everyone's stuck. Rabbit's working all the time, Dum and Dee won't get out of goal, Tortoise won't leave the house – Chatter makes a thousand plans and never follows them through – we need to break the loop.

   *(**ALICE** notices **CHATTER** has left her microphone on the seat. Slowly she walks towards it and picks it up.)*

ALICE. Testing. Testing. 1... 2... 3?
BREAK THE LOOP
OR THEY'LL NEVER STOP BEING COMMUTERS
BREAK THE LOOP
I THINK I KNOW HOW TO DO THIS!

COME ON LET'S DO THIS BREAK THE LOOP
AND CHANGE YOUR FUTURES IF NOT THINGS
WILL STAY THE SAME AND YOU'LL FOREVER BE
 COMMUTERS.

BREAK THE HABIT RABBIT LOOK AWAY FROM YOUR
COMPUTER
WORKING HARD IS A GOOD ROUTINE BUT REST YOUR
 EYES WHEN LOOKING AT SCREENS.

IT'S UNDERSTANDABLE, YOU'RE A BUSY ANIMAL
THE JOYS OF LIFE WILL PASS YOU BY IF YOU'RE STUCK
 DOWN A RABBIT HOLE.

*(**RABBIT** wakes up.)*

ALICE & RABBIT.
BREAK THE LOOP
CHANGE TRACK AND CHANGE OUR FUTURES.
BREAK THE LOOP
COME ON EVERYONE LET'S DO THIS!

ALICE.
NOW FOR TWEEDLE DEE
WE CAN FIX THIS EASILY
KICK THAT BALL BETWEEN YOUR FEET AND
YOU'LL RECOVER SPEEDILY
PASS THAT BALL TO TWEEDLE DUM,
DON'T MATTER WHO LOST OR WON
COMPETITION IS OKAY BUT THE AIM OF THE
GAME IS HAVING FUN.

*(**DEE** wakes up.)*

TORTOISE PLEASE COME OUT YOUR SHELL
DON'T STAY INSIDE ALL SAD AND BLUE
THE WORLD CAN BE A SCARY PLACE BUT
ALSO BRIGHT AND MAGICAL!
IF YOU FEEL AFRAID OF CHANGE REMEMBER
YOU'RE ADAPTABLE
COME ON LET'S GET OFF THIS TRAIN AND FIND
ELECTRIC AVENUE!

*(**TORTOISE** wakes up.)*

ALICE, TORTOISE & DEE.
BREAK THE LOOP
CHANGE TRACK AND CHANGE OUR FUTURES.
BREAK THE LOOP
COME ON EVERYONE LET'S DO THIS!

CHATTER. What are you doing with my mic?

ALICE. I had a few things to say.

CHATTER. Looks like you fixed everything then, you don't need me.

ALICE. Wait Chatter.
CHATTER! YOU, NOSE RAT AND PIGEON NEED
TO LEARN TO MAKE DECISIONS.
IF YOU DON'T TAKE THE FIRST STEP YOU'LL
NEVER COMPLETE A MISSION
ORGANISE ALL YOUR IDEAS AND YOU'LL
BECOME MORE PRACTICAL
THERE'S NO REWARD WITHOUT A RISK, LET'S
DO THE UNIMAGINABLE.

*(**PIGEON** wakes up.)*

PIGEON. I never did like that tea… CHATTER!

CHATTER & PIGEON. ALL CHANGE!

(The plastic rat and nose begin to rumble.)

PIGEON. They're... they're vibrating!

> (**PIGEON** *throws the objects away – and they transform! Into* **RAT** *and* **NOSE***!*)

I thought I'd lost you all forever!

RAT. Oh Pidge it was so scary in there, it was like looking into the great void beyond, it was nothing and everything at the same time, oh, the pull of the great endless nothing –

PIGEON. Rat. I could listen to you for hours.

> (**NOSE** *sprays.*)

BOTH. Peppermint!

PIGEON. Wait - I have a plan

> (*They plan in a huddle.*)

ALICE. Cat. CAT. I need you!

> (**CAT**'s *voice on the tannoy.*)

CAT. I'm *not* coming out.

ALICE. You don't have to. I need you to broadcast this to every single person on the train. Can you do that?

CAT. I've never done something like that before.

Let me see –

> (*One phone in the audience goes: Meow!*)

That's one. Now to expand the network...

> (*And another. And another. Phones going off all around the audience.*)

ALICE. Attention Commuters – can you hear me? I said – can you hear me?

AUDIENCE. *YES.*

ALICE. Then SING ALONG!

ALL.
>BREAK THE LOOP
>CHANGE TRACK AND CHANGE OUR FUTURES.
>BREAK THE LOOP
>COME ON EVERYONE LET'S DO THIS!
>
>BREAK THE LOOP
>CHANGE TRACK AND CHANGE OUR FUTURES.
>BREAK THE LOOP
>COME ON EVERYONE LET'S DO THIS!
>
>BREAK THE LOOP BREAK THE LOOP BREAK THE LOOP BREAK THE LOOP
>SAID BREAK THAT LOOP.
>
>BREAK THE LOOP BREAK THE LOOP BREAK THE LOOP BREAK THE LOOP
>SAID BREAK THAT LOOP!
>
>BREAK THE LOOP BREAK THE LOOP BREAK THE LOOP BREAK THE LOOP SAID BREAK THAT LOOP.
>
>BREAK THE LOOP BREAK THE LOOP BREAK THE LOOP BREAK THE LOOP
>SAID BREAK THAT LOOP!

ALICE. I have a plan.

>*(They all whisper something but **RABBIT** is hesitant.)*

RABBIT. I think you've got the wrong Rabbit.

ALICE. Rabbit I believe in you. Show them who's Boss!

Four

>(**DISTRICT** *and* **CIRCLE** *on patrol.* **RABBIT** *rushes in.*)

BOTH. Northolt!

RABBIT. You're much scarier than I remember.

DISTRICT. Poor little Bunny, maybe he should hop back to his Warren Street.

RABBIT. Right… well… erm.. what I have to say is very… erm… important… yes.

CIRCLE. Speak or we'll spike.

BOTH. Turnpike!

>*(They brandish their spears.)*

3, 2, 1…

RABBIT. WAIT! Have you ever considered strike action?

CIRCLE. What, you mean like hitting things?

DISTRICT. No, he's talking about bowling.

RABBIT. No, like not turning up for work, look here's a pamphlet. Be your own Boss, demand change! The Queen isn't in charge, you are.

DISTRICT. You mean…

BOTH. No more maintenance!? Tell us more!

>(**CHATTER** *and* **RABBIT** *enter.*)

CHATTER. Everyone's on board Alice, the plan's are working!

ALICE. Great, so we need to capture the Jabberwocky, show me what you've got?

CHATTER. What have I got?

ALICE. Yeah.

(The actor playing **CHATTER** *improvises three bizarre plans.)*

ALICE. Chatter they all sound great, just pick one.

CHATTER. One? Just one?... I know what to do.

*(***CHATTER*** exits.)*

ALICE. Wait Chatter, what is it?

*(***DUM*** and* **DEE** *come forward:)*

BOTH. HAMMERSMITH!

*(***HAMMERSMITH*** stomps out, holding his massive hammer...)*

HAMMERS. *What.*

DEE. Play us a game?

HAMMERS. I don't play games.

BOTH. You'll like this one, it's footy!

HAMMERS. I said, I don't play games.

BOTH. Why?

HAMMERS. Because I don't know how to play. They only ever want me to be big and scary and hit things. So no-one's ever played with me before.

DUM. That's alright.

DEE. The thing about football is...

BOTH. ...you always play as a team!

DUM. Come on, let's give Hammers a free kick.

HAMMERS. How do I play?

DEE. You kick it! Like this!

*(***HAMMERSMITH*** kicks the ball. They head off together singing.)*

Five

*(**CHATTER** rus in.)*

CHATTER. Alice, the plan's worked! The Jabberwocky's here!

ALICE. It's here! What do we do next?

CHATTER. Ermm… I didn't think that far ahead…

*(The **JABBERWOCKY** enters.)*

CHATTER. It's much bigger than I thought, but you've got this yeah Alice?

*(**CHATTER** runs away. The **JABBERWOCKY** roars and grows in size.)*

ALICE. Wait. Chatter. Wait.

The more you run away from it… the bigger it gets.

*(**ALICE** remembers **TORTOISE**.)*

TORTOISE. *(As a memory.) The more you run away from problems, the bigger they get.*

ALICE. Like a problem… Like a *problem*!

*(**ALICE** works up the courage.)*

JABBERWOCKY! I'M COMING TOWARDS YOU!

*(**ALICE** runs toward **JABBERWOCKY**.)*

(It shrinks and shrinks until…)

*(It is a tiny little **JABBERWOCKY**!)*

Wow. You really were more manageable than I thought.

Nice to meet you. I'm Alice, what's your name.

JABBER. Jabber. Jabber Wocky.

>(**JABBERWOCKY** *extends a claw and shakes* **ALICE***'s hand. He hops onto* **TORTOISE***'s shoulder.)*

TORTOISE. Aren't you a dear little thing.

ALICE. I thought you were a memory?

TORTOISE. Oh no, I've been standing here the whole time.

(To **JABBERWOCKY***.)* I'm going to feed you up. Plenty of beans on toast.

>*(***JABBERWOCKY** *gulps.)*

>*(***CHATTER** *runs in.)*

CHATTER. Alice! That was amazing! You're so brave.

ALICE. Chatter where did you go? You missed all the fun.

CHATTER. I'm so lucky to have you, you're my Angel.

(They hug.)

ALICE. I miss this.

I miss...

Six

PIGEON. Alice, we did it! We broke into the Queen's throne room, the rest is up to you. We're throwing the Queen in the gap.

> *(The **NOSE** sprays a vial.)*

Engine oil! Vroom Vroom. Engine oil! Vroom Vroom. Come on Chatter.

CHATTER. Come on Alice, Let's go!

> *(**CHATTER** exits.)*

ALICE. Wait, Tortoise. There's something I need.

TORTOISE. Are you sure? There are other ways.

ALICE. It's the only way.

> *(The vorpal sword emerges from a seating bank. **ALICE** walks over and picks it up.)*

I've got this.

TORTOISE. I know you do, good luck Alice.

ALICE.
ALICE-TOCRACY, ALICE -STOCRACY,
I'M THE QUEEN OF THE SOUND NO-ONES STOPPIN' ME.

> *(The cheering gets louder and louder.)*

> *(Then they step through into the **QUEEN**'s carriage.)*

Seven

(The **QUEEN***'s carriage. But* **CHATTER** *is gone.)*

ALICE. Queen, Queen. Where are you?

(A long slow laugh.)

QUEEN. You're supposed to be in the Gap.

ALICE. Show your face.

QUEEN. You don't give up, do you. Always breaking the rules, and rules are there for a reason.

ALICE. What.. are you scared of the Overgrounder?

QUEEN. Scared, I'm not scared of anything.

ALICE. Let the Chatter drive!

QUEEN. I'm afraid I'm what the train needs right now.

ALICE. That's not TRUE.

QUEEN. Yes it is.

ALICE. No it's not.

QUEEN. Yes it is

ALICE. No it's not.

QUEEN. Stop, we don't do that here.

QUEEN. Guards! Guards!! Guards?

ALICE. They're not coming.

QUEEN. Jabberwocky!

JABBERWOCKY.

(Nothing.)

Right. I see.

*(The **QUEEN** emerges. **ALICE** draws her sword.)*

ALICE. You don't belong here,'m throwing you in the Gap.

QUEEN. I don't want to do this Alice.

ALICE. We're *doing it.*

QUEEN. Very well. Prepare to meet your maker. Meet me on top of the train.

(They step on top of the train. Wind. Lights flashing past.)

ALICE. You've been lying to us. You're sending us round in a loop. And you hurt my friends…

QUEEN. You don't know what you're saying.

ALICE. There's only one place for you.

QUEEN. And where's that Alice?

Sitting in your bedroom writing your lyrics?

*(**ALICE** struggles to respond.)*

What are you saying? Use your English.

ALICE. *JUST SHUT UP!*

QUEEN. Guess this is a battle then.

BOTH. AAAAAAAAAAAAAAAA.

QUEEN. Don't get Osterley with me you Croxley little flea.

ALICE. I'm a power station mate, I'll send you to Battersea.

QUEEN. I'll cut in you two like Highbury and Islington.

ALICE. I'll knock you back and forth like it was Wimbledon!

QUEEN. You'll be MarleyBONES when I'm finished.

ALICE. My Cutty Sark will leave you diminished.

QUEEN. X marks the spot so prepare for my Brent Cross.

ALICE. I'll give you the wry-slip.

QUEEN. I'll Fairlop your head off.

ALICE. I'll puncture your Paddington – my Stratford is red hot!

QUEEN. This train terminates here and you'll never get off!

> *(The **QUEEN** gets the advantage. But then the digital **CAT** appears, and rings her phone.)*

One second I've got a notification...

CAT. Meow.

QUEEN. AH! CAT!

> *(**ALICE** fights back.)*

(Shouting over the noise of the train.) You just don't give up, do you.

ALICE. You're sending everyone in circles.

QUEEN. Well that's life isn't it! We're all going in circles.

> *(They battle. **ALICE** nearly falls off the train but regains her balance.)*

Careful!

ALICE. You're not my Mum! *(With every swing.)* STOP. TELLING. ME. WHAT. TO. DO.

QUEEN. I'm TRYING MY BEST.

ALICE. I HATE YOU.

> *(**ALICE** forces the **QUEEN** to the edge of the train. She holds the sword over her.)*

QUEEN. Go on. Do it. Throw me in.

(**QUEEN** *sniffles.*)

ALICE. What are you doing?

QUEEN. Nothing. I'm – I'm not doing anything –

ALICE. You're crying.

QUEEN. I'm not.

ALICE. You… are.

(**QUEEN** *cries.* **ALICE** *drops the sword.*)

Hey. Hey. What's wrong.

QUEEN. I don't know what to do. I'm just trying to keep everyone safe.

ALICE. Let's slow down. Let's stop.

QUEEN. No, we can't slow down, that's the problem. The train is BROKEN. All the controls are stuck. I can't change direction. It keeps speeding up and going round and round and round. I don't know what to do.

ALICE. Show me. I can help you.

QUEEN. I don't know if I can get up.

(**ALICE** *reaches out her hand.*)

ALICE. *Hold my hand.*

(*The* **QUEEN** *grasps it.*)

Eight

ALICE. Show me the driver's seat.

*(The **QUEEN** leads **ALICE** into the drivers seat. The driver's stick is thrust firmly in one direction.)*

QUEEN. See, I told you, the controls are stuck and we keep going round in circles.

*(**ALICE** tries to pull it back. It's stuck.)*

ALICE. With me. Pull it with me.

QUEEN. No.

ALICE. Queen.

QUEEN. YES. OKAY. YES.

(They both try. Nothing.)

I told you. It won't budge.

ALICE. I'll get the others. *(Calling.) EVERYONE.*

QUEEN. Don't let them in here, they'll make everything worse.

ALICE. We need help.

QUEEN. They'll think I'm weak.

ALICE. It doesn't make you weak, you can't do this on your own.

(Beat.)

QUEEN. Fine, they can come in.

(Tannoy) Everyone, this is your Queen speaking, I need help.

*(**TORTOISE** bursts through)*

TORTOISE. What do you need?

ALICE. Tortoise, what have you got in that pack?

TORTOISE. Just the thing!

>(**TORTOISE** *pulls out a rope, and attaches it to the stick.*)

>(**RABBIT** *bursts through too.*)

RABBIT. What do you need?

ALICE. All that energy, Rabbit. Use it. Run this rope back to everyone in the train.

RABBIT. Right away!

>(**RABBIT** *grabs the rope and runs off.*)

ALICE. And I need Dum and Dee working together!

>(**CAT** *wanders in.*)

CAT. Can I help…?

ALICE. Cat. You came.

CAT. I was thinking about what you said earlier about your school. I think I did let that worry get too big in my head – and this is much more important.

ALICE. Cat. Meet Queen.

QUEEN. Ergh, Cat!

CAT. Hello.

QUEEN. You're very handsome aren't you.

CAT. Thanks!? Gosh! Er!

Let me plug in –

>(**CAT** *plugs his laptop into the drivers' seat and begins to type.*)

ALICE. Three two one, PULL!

(They all pull – it's still stuck. The control desk starts to smoke.)

QUEEN. We're doomed.

CAT. None of my computers are working. I can't access anything. It's not behaving anything like a real train.

ALICE. Not like a real train?

CAT. No, it's like it's… alive.

TORTOISE. I told you she's a good girl!

ALICE. Smoke…

CAT. What?

ALICE. A long… winding…

There's someone missing. From the book, there's someone missing.

QUEEN. What are you on about now?

ALICE. This isn't a train. It's the Caterpillar!

QUEEN. HA! Impossible! You're joking!

DUM. *(From far away.) SHE'S NOT!*

DEE. *(From far away.) SHE IS!*

QUEEN. So, what do we do?

ALICE. We talk to it! That's how we break the loop. We stop for a second. Talk it out.

QUEEN. You've got to be kidding me.

*(**ALICE** approaches the controls.)*

ALL. HELLO? HELLO?

QUEEN. Hello is anyone there?

*(An adrenaline fuelled voice coming from the **TRAIN** itself.)*

TRAIN. HELLO!

QUEEN. We need to stop going faster!

TRAIN. FASTER? OKAY!

*(The **TRAIN** speeds up. Everyone screams! **ALICE** takes over.)*

ALICE. ARE YOU A CATERPILLAR?

TRAIN. HOW DID YOU KNOW?

QUEEN. You have GOT to be kidding me.

ALICE. WE NEED YOU TO STOP.

TRAIN. WHY WOULD I DO THAT! I'M HAVING THE TIME OF MY LIFE!

ALICE. Yes, but, you see, from – from our perspective you're going very fast, and we've been on here for a long time… and we'd love a break. If that's OK with you?

TRAIN. OH! I SEE! OF COURSE! I WISH YOU'D SAID SOMETHING SOONER. I NEVER SAW IT FROM THAT POINT OF VIEW!

VERY GLAD WE TALKED ABOUT IT.

ALICE. Me too.

QUEEN. It was that simple?

TRAIN. I'D HOLD ON TO SOMETHING IF I WERE YOU. TELL ME WHEN YOU'RE READY.

ALICE. What happens when we stop?

RABBIT. I don't know… we've never stopped.

TORTOISE. I suppose it's time to find out.

RABBIT. Thank you Alice! A – a pleasure.

TORTOISE. Thank you dear.

ALICE. I loved meeting you all. Friends are out there, aren't they, Cat?

CAT. You've just got to come out your shell.

TORTOISE. Oh shut up.

ALICE. Wait where's Queen? Where's Chatter?

TRAIN. HERE WE GO THEN!

THREE!

TWO!

ONE!

ALL. AAAAAAAAA!

(Screech.)

Nine

>*(Darkness. It feels like we're back in the Gap.)*

ALICE. I'm... No. I'm in the Gap!?

>*(**MUM** is there on the other side of the darkness.)*

Please. Please – don't – don't – AAA!

>*(She stalks toward **ALICE**. **ALICE** is terrified... then **MUM** embraces **ALICE** in a hug.)*

>*(We're on a station platform. **MUM** is all tears.)*

MUM. You are in *so much trouble.*

ALICE. It's you. It's YOU.

>*(**ALICE** kisses **MUM**'s cheek and hugs her tight.)*

MUM. What's this?

ALICE. And you're not gonna put me in the – in the – *in the Gap?*

MUM. What are you talking about?

ALICE. Did you miss me? Were you looking for me?

MUM. Alice...

ALICE. There was a Queen and a tortoise and a cat and – a weird – nose-man–thing – *(To herself.)* that was really strange – I'm so glad it's you.

MUM. *What are you talking about?*

ALICE. How long has it been?

MUM. Three minutes.

ALICE. I – I. *Noooo... Nooo!* It wasn't a dream. *NO.*

MUM. Come on. Get on.

(The train pulls in and they get on and sit down.)

Honestly I have no idea what you're talking about sometimes.

ALICE. It was, uh... it was...

*(**MUM** scrolls on her phone.)*

It was nothing. Nothing.

MUM. Well, if you're not going to talk to me, don't.

ALICE. I didn't... mean...

MUM. We're having a serious conversation when we get home, I hope you know that.

*(**ALICE** goes quiet.)*

And if you ignore me, or you're shutting your door, I'm taking away phone privileges. Silent treatment? Seriously... I give up.

*(**ALICE** huffs. **MUM** huffs. **MUM** is a little tearful.)*

ALICE. Are you... Mum, are you OK?

MUM. I'm fine.

ALICE. Because last week. In the recording room. I heard you... crying.

MUM. I – I... Alice.

I didn't know you saw that.

MUM. I was having a bad day.

ALICE. Just a bad day?

MUM. Well, it's been a hard few years hasn't it. I mean – lockdown together – *(Trying to laugh.)*, your Dad and I, I mean, you must be totally fed up of me.

ALICE. No.

MUM. And... and... I know I get on your nerves at the moment, but I have to right now... and we need rules, and boundaries, and you can't run off like that –

ALICE. I'm not asking that. I'm asking if...

MUM. What?

(**ALICE** *takes a deep breath.*)

ALICE. I'm trying to ask if you're okay.

MUM. Am I okay?

ALICE. Yeah, I wanna know? What's wrong?

MUM. I'm fine Alice. I'm fine. I mean, yes there's a lot in the air at the moment, and I know you find Nani a bit old fashioned – but it's Christmas, and she's – she's *consistent*, and I thought it would be nice to feel like everything was normal again for a minute. And I know she talks your ear off but she's been through a lot. And she's a good Mum. And I want to be a good Mum too. Sometimes I think I should be a bit more like her –

ALICE. You want to be like Nani?

MUM. No. Yes. No...

She *is* a good cook...

Ignore me. *Chatting on...* it's just sometimes...

(**ALICE** *hugs* **MUM**.)

ALICE. Sometimes there's just... just a lot of nonsense to deal with.

MUM. Exactly. You try to make it all – it all work. Try to make sense of everything and... a lot of the time... like you said it's just nonsense. We're just...

ALICE. Living through the nonsense.

MUM. Exactly.

That's very mature.

ALICE. Yeah well I am eleven.

MUM. You are.

> *(Then suddenly –* **MUM** *sees something across the seats.)*
>
> *Is that a turtle?*
>
> *(A* **TORTOISE** *crawls towards them across the seats.)*
>
> WHAT'S IT DOING ON THE VICTORIA LINE!

ALICE. It's a tortoise.

MUM. How do you know that?

ALICE. Hands not flippers.

> *(***ALICE*** shows* **MUM** *the* **TORTOISE.***)*

MUM. Don't, it makes me feel guilty. I left one of those on a train once, I was so upset when I got home – you're not taking her home are you?

ALICE. I'm showing her Brixton. Please please please – I'm taking her to see Nani.

MUM. Alright, well you're looking after her, not me. Whatever they eat. Celery.

ALICE. Baked beans, actually.

ANNOUNCER. Good evening. Just a note to say any unattended baggage will be taken by the conductor and sold on eBay.

ANNOUNCER 2. You can't say that!

ANNOUNCER. What's wrong with a bit of magic on the mic?

ANNOUNCER 2. Well I suppose it is the season to be jolly.

ANNOUNCER. Next station Vauxhall. Vauxhall. Merry Christmas, and a Happy New Year.

    (**MUM** *laughs.*)

MUM. I didn't know tubes had co-pilots.

    (**ALICE** *plays a song in her headphones.*)

ALICE.
    ALICE-TOCRACY, ALICE-TOCRACY, I'M THE QUEEN OF THE SOUND /NO-ONE'S STOPPIN' ME.

MUM. So what's the latest bars then?

    (**ALICE** *smiles and offers* **MUM** *a headphone.*)

    (**MUM** *puts it in, the music swells.*)

ALICE. Ah Mum, come on... So, it goes –
    ALICE-TOCRACY, ALICE-TOCRACY, I'M THE QUEEN OF THE SOUND /NO-ONE'S STOPPIN' ME.

MUM. It's not all about *you* you know.

ALICE. I know! That's not what it's about –

MUM. Well you clearly think it is.

ALICE. ... So what have you got then?

MUM. What? Is this a battle?

ALICE. Yeah.

MUM. Okay, you start.

ALICE.
>ALICE-TOCRACY, ALICE-STOCRACY,
>I'M THE QUEEN OF THE SOUND NO-ONES STOPPIN' ME.
>ALICE-TOCRACY, ALICE-STOCRACY,
>I'M THE BEST AND THERE'S NO MEDIOCRITY.

MUM.
>MUMMYSTOCRACY, MUMMYSTOCRACY,
>I'M NOT SURE IF I'M DOING THIS PROPERLY
>MUMMYSTOCRACY, MUMMYSTOCRACY,
>IT'S OKAY, AS LONG AS I'M ON THE BEAT.

ALICE. YES!
>EVERYONE LISTEN UP GATHER ROUND
>I AM THE BRAND NEW ACTON TOWN
>SOON I'LL BE BIGGER THAN MANOR HOUSE
>I'VE GOT MORE LINES THAN THE UNDERGROUND
>THAT'S GOSPEL OAK YOU CAN'T HACKNEY DOWNS
>GOT WAY MORDEN CAMDEN TOWN
>GET ON YOUR NEASDEN YOU HAVE TO BOW
>ELIZABETH LINE? I HAVE THE CROWN!

Go!

MUM.
>NOW THAT I'VE GOT TO A DECENT START
>I CAN EXPLORE THIS LIKE REGENT'S PARK
>THIS IS A COOL WAY TO TALK TO YOU
>I GUESS WE'RE CONNECTING LIKE WATERLOO
>FIGHTING THE QUEENSWAY SERVED ITS TIME
>WE BROKE THE LOOP ON THE CIRCLE LINE
>WE CAN STOP BARKING THE WORLD IS FINE
>THERE'S A BRAND NEW START ON THE PURPLE LINE.
>
>MUMMYSTOCRACY, MUMMYSTOCRACY,
>BOND STREET FOR A CHRISTMAS SHOPPING SPREE
>MUMMYSTOCRACY, MUMMYSTOCRACY,
>DON'T LAUGH, THIS ISN'T A COMEDY!

ALICE.
>ALICE-TOCRACY, ALICE-STOCRACY,
>I'M THE QUEEN OF THE SOUND NO-ONES STOPPIN' ME.
>ALICE-TOCRACY, ALICE-STOCRACY,

BOTH.
>I'M THE BEST AND THERE'S NO MEDIOCRITY.
>YEAH!

ABOUT POLTERGEIST

Poltergeist are an award-winning group of directors, writers, designers and performers who come together to make theatre. Named "one of the UK's best young theatre companies" by the Guardian, they make work that is, first and foremost, collaborative, and fully in touch with all aspects of design. They are Associate Company at the Rose Theatre, Kingston, Creative Associates at The North Wall, Oxford, and one of New Diorama Theatre's supported companies.

www.ingramcontent.com/pod-product-compliance
Ingram Content Group UK Ltd.
Pitfield, Milton Keynes, MK11 3LW, UK
UKHW021840210426
5322IPUK00022B/384